★STUDY GUIDES

Science

Year 6

**Alan Jarvis and
William Merrick**

RISING★STARS

Rising Stars UK Ltd, 22 Grafton Street, London W1S 4EX

www.risingstars-uk.com

Published 2007
Text, design and layout © Rising Stars UK Ltd.

Design: HL Studios
Illustrations: Aptara Inc., New Delhi, India
Editorial project management: Dodi Beardshaw
Editorial: Marieke O'Connor
Cover design: Burville-Riley Design

British Library Cataloguing in Publication Data.
A CIP record for this book is available from the British Library.

ISBN: 978-1-84680-103-7

Printed by: Gutenberg Press, Malta.

Contents

How to get the best out of this book

Each topic spreads across two pages and focuses on one major idea. Many of your lessons may be based on these topics. Each double page helps you to 'keep on track' and to 'aim higher'.

Title and key ideas: tell you what you are aiming to learn. The second idea is always more difficult than the first.

Key information: sets out the key facts that you need to know and the ideas you need to understand fully.

Key questions: help you to learn more facts and understand the science in each topic. The investigations you do will give you the evidence you need to prove the scientific facts you've learned.

Key words and their meanings: help build up your scientific vocabulary. Remember that some words mean one thing in everyday life and something more special in science.

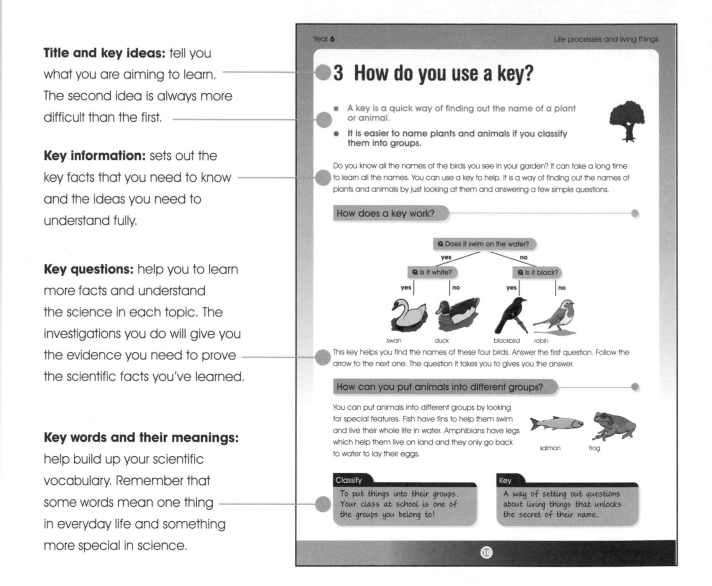

Year **6**   Life processes and living things

3 How do you use a key?

- A key is a quick way of finding out the name of a plant or animal.
- It is easier to name plants and animals if you classify them into groups.

Do you know all the names of the birds you see in your garden? It can take a long time to learn all the names. You can use a key to help. It is a way of finding out the names of plants and animals by just looking at them and answering a few simple questions.

How does a key work?

Q Does it swim on the water?
yes / no
Q Is it white? / Q Is it black?
yes | no / yes | no

swan   duck   blackbird   robin

This key helps you find the names of these four birds. Answer the first question. Follow the arrow to the next one. The question it takes you to gives you the answer.

How can you put animals into different groups?

You can put animals into different groups by looking for special features. Fish have fins to help them swim and live their whole life in water. Amphibians have legs which help them live on land and they only go back to water to lay their eggs.

salmon   frog

Classify
To put things into their groups. Your class at school is one of the groups you belong to!

Key
A way of setting out questions about living things that unlocks the secret of their name.

⑩

Follow these simple rules if you are using the book for revising.

1 Read each page carefully. Give yourself time to take in each idea.

2 Learn the key facts and ideas. Ask your teacher or mum, dad or the adult who looks after you if you need help.

3 Concentrate on the things you find more difficult.

4 Only work for about 20 minutes or so at a time. Take a break and then do more work.

The right-hand page has lots of fun questions for you to try. They are like the National Curriculum test questions you will do. The answers are in the pull-out section in the middle of this book.

If you get most of the On track questions right, you know you are working at level 4. Well done – that's brilliant! If you get most of the Aiming higher questions right, you are working at the higher level 5. You're really doing well!

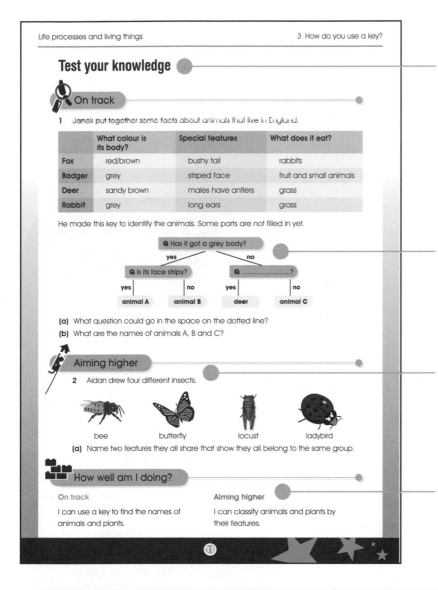

SAT-style questions: help you to find out how well you have understood what you have learnt. There are questions on facts, ideas and scientific investigations. If you are stuck, the information on the left-hand page will help. **Write all your answers in your notebook.**

On track questions: come in different styles. Be sure to read each one carefully. Think about what the diagrams are telling you.

Aiming higher questions: are more difficult. To answer them well, you have to know more facts or understand a harder idea.

How well am I doing?: helps you to find out the level at which you are working. Keep a running record so you keep on target.

Follow these simple rules if you want to know how well you are doing.

1 Work through the questions.

2 Keep a record of how well you do.

3 If you are working at level 4 you will get most of the On track questions correct.

4 If you are working at level 5 you will also get most of the Aiming higher questions correct.

1 Why do plants need light?

- Plants need light, air (carbon dioxide) and water to grow.
- **Plants use light, air and water to make food for growth.**

What happens to the grass on a lawn if you cover it with a box or a stone? After one or two days it goes a pale yellow colour. Later on it might look completely dead. If you let light and air get to it, it soon comes back to a healthy green colour and starts to grow again.

What does a plant need to grow?

Plants need carbon dioxide. They get this from air. Tiny holes in the underside of the leaves let air in and out.

Plants need water. A plant will only live a few days without water. Roots take up the water which then goes to the rest of the plant. Plants need light. They take this in through the leaves.

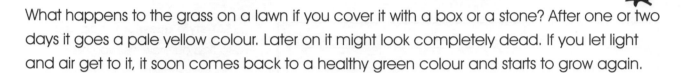

Leaves have a green chemical, called chlorophyll, which catches the light.

Why does a plant need carbon dioxide, water and light?

Plants need food to grow, the same as we do. We eat the food we need, but a plant cannot do that. It has no mouth and can grow without needing to eat at all!

Plants make their own food. All they need to do this is **carbon dioxide** from the air and **water**. They make food out of them, taking energy from sunlight.

The plant has made the food in these potatoes from carbon dioxide in the air and water.

Grow
To increase in size and weight.

Food
A source of energy and materials needed to grow.

Test your knowledge

On track

1   Aidan has been sleeping in a tent on his holiday.

When he packed up his tent to go home he noticed that the grass had gone yellow and was nearly dead underneath the tent.

(a) What had Aidan's tent done to stop the grass growing?

(b) What is the name of the green colour that should be in a leaf?

(c) What will happen to the grass now Aidan has moved his tent?

Aiming higher

Trees need plenty of light to make them grow properly.

(a) Name two other things that plants need to take in to grow.

(b) What does the plant do with those things it takes in?

(c) How does Aidan take in the things that he needs to grow?

How well am I doing?

On track

I can say why plants need light, air and water.

Aiming higher

I can explain that plants grow using food they have made themselves.

2 Why do plants need soil?

- Soil contains water and other nutrients that plants need.
- Different soils are suitable for different plants.

You know plants make their own food from air and water. Soil is still important to plants – some soils can be poor and not much can grow in it. Other soils are very good, and the garden plants grow well. So, what is it that makes a soil good or bad?

What is the soil needed for?

Plants could blow over, or be washed away by the rain. Roots hold them in place.

Soil contains water which plants need to make food. Roots have little hairs to soak up water from the soil.

Soil contains nutrients which the plant needs. Farmers and gardeners add these chemicals to the soil as fertiliser. It makes their plants grow better. Manure is a good fertiliser!

Are some soils better than others?

Sand does not contain much dead animal or plant material. It has few nutrients. Not many plants grow well in sand!

Clay has tiny soil particles which stick together. There are few air spaces. Plants find it hard to grow in it. Loamy garden soil is excellent. It has air spaces which let roots grow well. Digging the soil puts more air spaces in it.

sandy soil

Rotting leaves give the soil nutrients. They also soak up water and stop it drying out.

clay soil

Nutrients

Chemicals in the soil that a plant needs to grow properly.

loamy soil

Fertiliser

Anything that improves soil by adding nutrients.

Test your knowledge

 On track

1 Miss Harper likes gardening. Tasty vegetables grow in her garden's excellent soil.

Here are four things a plant needs.

water   carbon dioxide   fertiliser   something for the roots to hold on to

(a) Which of these things is not provided by the soil?

(b) What can Miss Harper add to her soil to make it have more nutrients for her plants?

Aiming higher

1 Look at these two plants. Think about what they need.

bluebells

oak tree

(a) Which plant needs the strongest roots?

(b) Which plant does not need much sunlight?

 How well am I doing?

On track

I can say what the soil gives to a plant.

Aiming higher

I can explain why different plants live in different places.

3 How do you use a key?

- **A key is a quick way of finding out the name of a plant or animal.**

- **It is easier to name plants and animals if you classify them into groups.**

Do you know all the names of the birds you see in your garden? It can take a long time to learn all the names. You can use a key to help. It is a way of finding out the names of plants and animals by just looking at them and answering a few simple questions.

How does a key work?

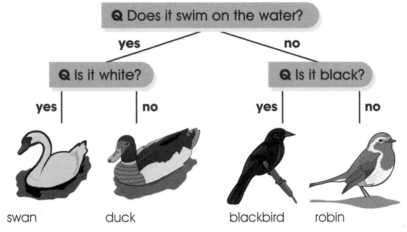

Q Does it swim on the water?

yes — **Q Is it white?**   no — **Q Is it black?**

yes   no   yes   no

swan   duck   blackbird   robin

This key helps you find the names of these four birds. Answer the first question. Follow the arrow to the next one. The question it takes you to gives you the answer.

How can you put animals into different groups?

You can put animals into different groups by looking for special features. Fish have fins to help them swim and live their whole life in water. Amphibians have legs which help them live on land and they only go back to water to lay their eggs.

salmon   frog

Classify

To put things into their groups. Your class at school is one of the groups you belong to!

Key

A way of setting out questions about living things that unlocks the secret of their name.

Test your knowledge

On track

1   Janek put together some facts about animals that live in England.

	What colour is its body?	Special features	What does it eat?
Fox	red/brown	bushy tail	rabbits
Badger	grey	striped face	fruit and small animals
Deer	sandy brown	males have antlers	grass
Rabbit	grey	long ears	grass

He made this key to identify the animals. Some parts are not filled in yet.

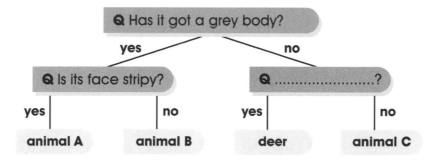

(a) What question could go in the space on the dotted line?

(b) What are the names of animals A, B and C?

Aiming higher

2   Aidan drew four different insects.

bee   butterfly   locust   ladybird

(a) Name two features they all share that show they all belong to the same group.

How well am I doing?

On track

I can use a key to find the names of animals and plants.

Aiming higher

I can classify animals and plants by their features.

4 Who eats who?

- Food chains show what different animals eat.
- Green plants make all the food in the first place.

Say you eat an egg for breakfast which gives you lots of energy. The egg was made by a hen, using energy she got from her food – grains like wheat and barley. Those come from green grasses that grow in the sunshine. That means you must be living on sunshine!

What does a plant need to grow?

Jaden's **food chain** shows that the fox eats the rabbit, and the rabbit eats the grass.

grass	→	rabbit	→	fox
producer		consumer		consumer

The grass is called a **producer** because it makes (produces) the food in the first place. The rabbit and the fox are both **consumers**. They eat (consume) something else, to live.

Why does a food chain always start with a green plant?

Green plants do not need to eat something else. They make the food for everything else.

Even a lion, which only eats meat, needs the food produced by the grass. The animals he eats all eat grass.

Producer

A green plant which makes its own food using sunlight energy.

Consumer

Animals are consumers because they eat green plants or other animals.

Test your knowledge

On track

1   Miss Harper's cat Billy has eaten a pigeon. The pigeon had been eating Miss Harper's bean plants. She is sad for the pigeon, but pleased for her beans.

(a) Make up a food chain to show what has happened.

⬚ ⟶ ⬚ ⟶ ⬚

(b) What is the producer in this food chain?

(c) Why is Billy called a consumer?

Aiming higher

2   In a wood there is an owl. The owl never eats green plants – it only ever eats meat. It catches mice and sometimes small birds.

(a) Explain why the plants in the wood do not need to eat anything.

(b) Why would the owl go hungry if the plants in the wood were not growing healthlly?

How well am I doing?

On track

I can show what animals eat in the form of a food chain.

Aiming higher

I can explain why all food chains start with a green plant.

5 How are living things adapted?

- Plants and animals have special features to help them survive.
- Different organisms are adapted to different habitats

All animals and plants have special ways of surviving in the place where they live. A fish has a tail to swim with; it is specially suited to live in the water. Bluebells are one of the first flowers to come out in the spring. They need to grow before the trees shade them.

How can animals and plants be specially adapted to survive?

The lion's colour helps it hide when it is hunting.

A flamingo's long legs help it to wade in the water.

How do the conditions affect where animals and plants live?

Camels are sandy-coloured so they blend into their surroundings. Their big feet stop them sinking into the soft sand.

All fish have gills to breathe under water. Their streamlined (pointed) shape means they can slip through the water quickly.

Suited
Having features that help plants and animals survive.

Adapted
Living things change over time to help them survive better.

Test your knowledge

On track

1   Mammoths were very much like elephants. They lived in cold and snowy places. They died out about 10,000 years ago.

(a) How were the mammoths specially suited to their cold environment?

(b) Elephants live in hot places. What is the elephant above doing to help it cope with the heat?

Aiming higher

2   Arctic foxes and polar bears like these live near the North Pole.

(a) Explain why these two animals are well suited to their environment.

(b) What problems might they have if they were living in warmer countries?

arctic fox   polar bear

How well am I doing?

On track

I can say how plants and animals are specially suited for survival.

Aiming higher

I can explain why different plants and animals live in different places.

6 What makes you ill?

- Illness is caused by very small organisms (germs) living inside us.

- **Scientists had to gather evidence to prove that germs cause illness.**

Why do you get ill? Some diseases are caused by tiny micro-organisms called **germs** living inside you. They are much too small to see normally, but they can be seen under a microscope. Wash those germs off before they get inside you!

What diseases are caused by microbes (germs)?

Some of Tiger class have been quite ill.

- Harry does not clean his teeth. The germs have built up and given him tooth decay.
- A germ has given Sam chicken pox. It has spread to her friend Annetta.
- Many of the boys have had a cold this winter. Sneezing spreads the germs.
- Jack forgot to wash his hands after going to the toilet. He has a poorly tummy.

How were germs discovered?

Edward Jenner was an English doctor.

In 1796 he noticed that people milking cows got blisters on their hands. They had caught a cow illness called cowpox.

He noticed something even more interesting. Those people never seemed to get a really serious human illness called smallpox. He gave a boy cowpox on purpose by injecting him with some liquid from the cowpox blisters.

Later on he actually tried to make him catch smallpox by injecting liquid from smallpox blisters!

Luckily the experiment had worked. The boy could not get smallpox. He was the first person ever to be vaccinated!

Micro-organisms
Tiny living things only seen with a microscope.

Germs
The everyday word for microbes that can make you ill.

Test your knowledge

On track

1   Many but not all illnesses are caused by germs. Some
    Tiger class children were off school. Asha had a cold.
    Linford had a broken leg. Jaden had a bad tooth. Aidan
    had chickenpox.

(a) Which child's absence was not caused by germs?

(b) What could Jaden have done to stop herself getting a
     bad tooth?

(c) Why should you always wash your hands before eating?

Aiming higher

2   **Louis Pasteur** lived about 150 years ago. He studied what happens when
    sugary liquids ferment to make beer.
    • Gas bubbles are made and the sugar turns into alcohol.
    • Louis could see yeast microbes under his microscope when the yeast
      was fermenting.
    • If there wasn't any yeast the beer would not ferment.

(a) What did Louis' observations show? Pick the right one from this list.
     (i)   Yeast is killed by alcohol.
     (ii)   Yeast is needed to turn sugar into alcohol.
     (iii) Beer tastes of yeast.
     (iv)   Alcohol is bad for you.

(b) Microbes are killed by heat. Louis found he could stop milk going bad by heating
     it up. We call that **pasteurisation**. How did heating up the milk stop it going bad?

How well am I doing?

On track

I can say how some illnesses are caused
by microbes.

Aiming higher

I can describe some of the evidence
which shows germs cause disease.

7 Why does food go mouldy?

- Food goes mouldy and decays because of very small organisms.

- **Food poisoning is caused if germs spread from one food to another.**

Germs grow on food and feed on it. They spoil the food for us. A loaf of bread only lasts two or three days. Meat can go 'bad' in a day in warm weather. Bad food causes food poisoning. How can we keep our food safe?

Why do things go bad?

Mould has started to grow on the bread. It will have to be thrown away!

This fish has been dead too long – microbes have made it smell nasty.

Microbes make all dead things rot – the cat won't want to eat this bird.

How can you stop germs from spreading?

- 👍 Be hygienic!
- 👍 Wash your hands after you have been to the toilet, especially before touching food.
- 👍 Keeping the kitchen clean is important too. Knives, pots and pans carry germs.
- 👍 Keep food cool – germs need warmth.
- 👍 Keep those pets away from your food!

Decay
Decay is the correct name for rotting.

Hygiene
Hygiene means keeping clean, with no germs.

Test your knowledge

On track

1   Jaden and Aidan put some pieces of cheese in jam jars.
    They screwed the lids on tight and checked them every day
    for two weeks. The cheese became green and looked 'furry'.
    Then it went runny in the bottom of the jar. After that their
    teacher threw it away!

(a) What causes the cheese to go bad?

(b) Why did they keep the jars screwed up tight the whole time?

(c) Aidan remembered finding the skeleton of a dead bird in
         the woods. What had made all the soft parts 'disappear' so
         he could see the bones?

Aiming higher

2   Jaden's mum bought two loaves of bread on the same day. She put one in the
    bread bin and the other in the freezer. The loaf in the bread bin went mouldy after
    three days and they had to throw it away. The one in the freezer was still good.

(a) How do you think the mould got on the bread in the first place?

(b) Jaden thought the freezer kept the bread from going mouldy because it was so cold.
         Her mum thought it was the darkness in the freezer that stopped the mould from
         growing. Say who you think was right, and explain why.

How well am I doing?

On track

I can say that things go bad when
micro-organisms grow on them.

Aiming higher

I can explain some ways in which germs
get onto our food.

8 What micro-organisms can you eat?

- Some very small organisms are used to make food.

- We can prove that yeast, which we use to make bread, is alive.

Most people think of microbes as being bad things. This is because some of them cause diseases, and others make our food go bad. Some are very good for us, and help us to make food! You have probably already eaten thousands of good microbes today!

How can we use microbes to make food?

Microbes make yoghurt, cheese and bread.

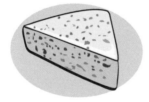

Some people say that the mould on this blue cheese makes it taste really nice.

A microbe called yeast makes bubbles in the dough.

How can you prove yeast is alive?

Yeast looks like lots of little light brown balls. It looks more like a chemical than a living thing. How do we know it is alive?

without sugar   with sugar

These two jars both contain yeast and water. One has some sugar in it, the other just has water. Both are kept warm. They must not be too hot or the yeast will be killed. After a little while, the mixture with sugar makes bubbles of gas because you have fed it. It is alive!

Dough
The paste of flour and water that we make bread from.

Fungus
A group that includes yeast, mushrooms and mould.

Test your knowledge

On track

1 Here are some foods from Asha's kitchen.

yoghurt

bread

butter

blue cheese

jam

honey

(a) Which foods are made using microbes?

(b) Why is yeast added to the dough when bread is made?

Aiming higher

2 Asha's bread dough is rising. Air bubbles appear. They are being made by the yeast which is in the dough. The dough contains sugar and yeast. It has to be kept warm or it will not rise.

(a) How can you prove that yeast is alive?

(b) If the dough was warmed up a few degrees what effect would it have on the rising of the dough? Explain your answer.

How well am I doing?

On track

I can say which foods are made using micro-organisms.

Aiming higher

I can give some evidence to show that yeast is alive.

9 Can you make dirty water clean?

- Sieves and filters are used to filter water.
- Dirty water can be partly cleaned by filtering.

Clean water is hard to find. Water in streams often has small pebbles or particles of soil mixed in with it. Dirty water can be made clear. Big particles can be sieved out. The smaller ones have to be removed using a process called **filtering**.

How can the big stones be removed?

This water looks dirty. Mixed in with it are stones and particles of different sizes. The first step in making it clearer is to pass everything though a sieve. Water and small particles pass through. The stones and larger particles stay in the sieve.

How can the smaller particles be removed?

The water still is not clear. What you need to do is to trap out the smallest particles. The next step is to fold a filter paper and put it into a filter funnel like in the diagram. When you pass the water through this the smaller particles stay in the paper. Clear water passes through into the beaker.

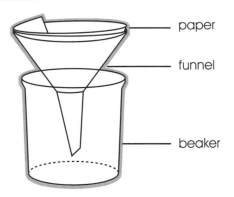

paper

funnel

beaker

Sieve
A strainer for separating particles from water or lumps from a powder.

Filter
A piece of equipment for separating small particles from a liquid.

Test your knowledge

On track

1   Tom looks around his house. He spots some sieves and filters.

colander   vacuum cleaner   sieve   coffee maker

(a) Sort the devices into sieves and filters.   **(b)** Say what the devices usually separate.

Aiming higher

2   Write these instructions in the correct order.

- Filter the sieved water.

- Collect the clean water in a beaker.

- Put the dirty water in a beaker.

- Put a folded filter paper in a funnel.

- Sieve the dirty water.

How well am I doing?

On track

I can say what sieving and filtering are used for.

Aiming higher

I can produce a flow chart to show how to make water clear.

10 Can you make dirty water pure?

- **Some water is purer than other water.**
- **You can predict the purity and test to see if you are right.**

Not all water is the same. Pure (distilled) water is just what it says: it only contains water. However, water often contains impurities. Other substances can dissolve in it. Even clear water may not be pure.

How pure is sea water?

Asha collected some clear sea water. Its salty taste told her that it was not pure.

She predicted that 'sea water contains a lot of salt'.

How can Asha see if her prediction is correct?

To see if the sea water has something dissolved in it, Asha needs a way of getting rid of the water.

Miss Harper suggests she puts some of her water in a dish on the radiator overnight to make the water evaporate.

She comes back in the morning and sees white powder in the dish.

Asha's prediction was right. Sea water contains salt.

Pure

In science, a substance which is free from any impurities.

Prediction

An informed idea of what will happen in an investigation.

Test your knowledge

  **On track**

1   Tiger class tests these four liquids to see how pure they are.

filtered pond water   lemonade   distilled water   tap water

(a)   Write down those which are impure.

(b)   Predict what would happen to each if you did Asha's test on each one.

 Aiming higher

2   Here are the Tiger class results.

	Filtered pond water	Lemonade	Distilled water	Tap water
What was in the dish in the morning?	quite a lot of dirty solid	a little white solid	nothing	tiny amount of a solid

(a)   Use the results to explain if your predictions were true or not.

(b)   Put the water in order of purity. Start with the purest first.

(c)   What do you think might be dissolved in the impure water(s)?

 How well am I doing?

On track

I can name three things that dissolve in water.

Aiming higher

I can test a prediction with an experiment.

11 How can you separate mixtures?

● Solids and liquids can be recovered from a solution by evaporation.

● A special form of this is called distillation.

Explorers need plenty of pure water to drink. Stream water needs purifying before they can drink it. A good way to do this is to warm up some water in a can. The evaporated water will condense on a cold surface. The water you collect is pure. The impurities stay in the can.

How can evaporation help separate solutions?

Miss Harper is heating some salty water. The water **evaporates**. Very hot steam comes off.

She has put a cold surface nearby. The hot steam hits it and **condenses**. This turns it back into liquid water. It drips off and can be collected in a beaker. The salt stays behind.

What equipment do scientists use to do this?

Miss Harper says 'scientists call this way of separating a liquid from a solution **distillation**'. To make it easier, they use this special apparatus.

If you distill salty water, pure water collects in the conical flask. Salt is left behind in the round-bottomed flask.

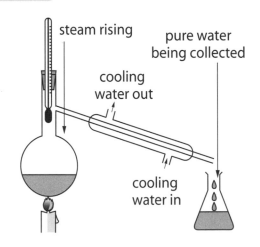

steam rising   pure water being collected

cooling water out

cooling water in

Evaporation
Changing a liquid into a gas, usually below its boiling point.

Distillation
The process of boiling a liquid and condensing its vapours.

Test your knowledge

On track

I think the steam from the blue ink will not be blue, because only the water evaporates.

1   Aidan uses the same method of evaporation as Miss Harper. He uses ink instead of salty water.
    He made this prediction.

(a) Copy and complete this table to show what Aidan observes.

Colour of the condensed steam	
Name of the substance in the beaker	
How does the ink colour change?	

Aiming higher

2   Aidan distills some other substances in distillation apparatus.

	Can be separated by distillation	Cannot be separated by distillation
Salty water		
Distilled water		
Tea		
Pure cooking oil		

(a) What two changes take place during distillation?

(b) Copy and complete the chart with ticks to show which substances can be separated.

(c) Explain each of your answers in (b). Make sentences with 'I think … because … '

How well am I doing?

On track

I can describe how evaporation helps separate a solution.

Aiming higher

I can explain the science behind distillation.

12 What are the rules of dissolving?

- **Fair tests help you investigate what speeds up dissolving.**

- **Reliable results help you write rules but some results might not fit.**

Think about how fast sugar dissolves in tea (water). Stirring, changing the size of the sugar crystals, the amount of water and its temperature might all have an effect. As scientists, you can do fair tests to find out the rules of dissolving.

How can you test one way of speeding up dissolving?

Jaden predicted 'sugar will dissolve quicker in hot water than cold water'.

- She changed the temperature of the water. She kept the volume of water and the amount and kind of sugar the same. She stirred her mixture.

- She timed how long it took for all the sugar to dissolve. She did three tests to make her results more reliable.

What results might you get?

These look OK. The hotter it is, the faster it dissolves

This doesn't fit the pattern. Do it again!

Temperature (°C)	Time in minutes		
	Test 1	Test 2	Test 3
30	14	15	14
40	12	13	18
50	11	11	11

Solution

A liquid that has a substance dissolved in it.

Anomalous result

A result that looks odd compared with the other results.

Test your knowledge

On track

1 Jaden decided to test whether the size of salt crystals affects the time it takes for the salt to dissolve. She used large crystals (rock salt), medium crystals (sea salt) and small crystals (table salt).

(a) What is the one factor she should change as she carries out this investigation?

(b) Name one of the factors she should keep the same to make this investigation fair.

Aiming higher

2 Here are Jaden's results.

Type of salt	Time in minutes to dissolve		
	Test 1	Test 2	Test 3
Rock salt	180	175	185
Sea salt	95	140	95
Table salt crystals	45	55	50

(a) Why did she do her second test three times?

(b) Which result looks odd (anomalous)?

(c) Pick the right rule from this list.

- The bigger the salt crystals, the faster they dissolve.
- The size of the salt crystals doesn't affect how fast they dissolve.
- The smaller the salt crystals, the faster they dissolve.

How well am I doing?

On track

I can say what speeds up dissolving.

Aiming higher

I can explain what to do when results look odd.

13 How do we use test results?

- **Fair tests help you investigate dissolving.**
- **Graphs can be used to make further predictions.**

Newsweet are testing their products. Miss Harper's class are interested in finding out the maximum amount of their new sweetener that will dissolve in water at different temperatures. Miss Harper's class are experts at drawing graphs.

How did Tiger class do their fair test on dissolving?

Tiger class measured how much sweetener dissolved in water at different temperatures. To make the test fair they used the same sweetener every time and the same amount of water.

What results did they get to help make their graph?

Once the class had decided correctly what to keep the same, what to change and what to measure, their test was fair. As you can see, the results of the groups differ. Some errors were made!

Temperature (°C)	Maximum amount of sugar that dissolves (g/50 cm³)			
	Group A	Group B	Group C	Group D
30	105	109	110	116
40	126	120	118	116
50	No results made			
60	133	142	140	145
70	156	166	158	160

Now they need to make a graph to show these more clearly.

Saturated solution

The most concentrated solution possible at a given temperature.

Error

A mistake. A wrong value recorded when measuring.

Test your knowledge

On track

1   Jaden decided to make a
    graph of the class results.
    She has made a start.

(a) Explain what a saturated
    solution is.

(b) Copy the graph and
    complete the scale for
    each axis.

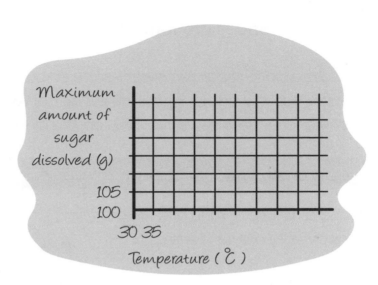

Aiming higher

2   Jaden had to do some more work before she could complete her graph.

(a) Use the results of the class to work out the average amount that dissolved for
    each temperature.

(b) Explain why it is best to work out an average if several sets of observations are made.

(c) Draw the graph, putting the temperatures on the x axis and the amounts that
    dissolved on the y axis.

(d) Use your graph to predict the maximum amount of sugar that will dissolve at 50°C in
    50 cm³ of water.

How well am I doing?

On track

I can describe how to do a fair test
on dissolving.

Aiming higher

I can present results in a graph and use it
to make a prediction.

14 Can changes be reversed?

- A mixture of substances can sometimes be separated easily.
- If new substances are formed we can't reverse it so easily.

Have you ever had to separate different-coloured building bricks that have got mixed up? That mix-up is easily reversible. What if the plastic got very hot and the bricks all melted together? That change is irreversible – you can't undo it once it has happened.

How can a mixture of substances be reversed?

Asha found a mixture of sand and iron filings was an easy one to reverse.

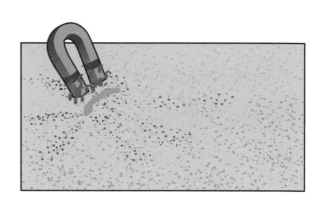

'A magnet will lift out the iron filings and leave the sand behind.'

What might show that a change is irreversible?

Asha added some vinegar to some bicarbonate of soda. New substances were made. She said, 'You can see bubbles of gas escaping. You cannot reverse this. The bubbles won't go back in!'

Vinegar

bicarbonate of soda

Mixture

When two or more substances are jumbled up together.

Reverse

To make a change go back to where it started.

RISING STARS

Science Study Guide: Year 6

Answer Booklet

Unit	On track: Q1		Aiming higher : Q2	
1 Why do plants need light?	**(a)**	Stopped the plant getting the light and water it needs to grow	**(a)**	Carbon dioxide and water
	(b)	Chlorophyll	**(b)**	Makes food out of them
	(c)	The grass will grow again	**(c)**	Eating food through his mouth
2 Why do plants need soil?	**(a)**	Carbon dioxide	**(a)**	An oak tree
	(b)	Fertiliser or manure	**(b)**	Bluebell(s)
3 How do you use a key?	**(a)**	Does it eat grass?	**(a)**	They all have wings / They all have three parts to their bodies
	(b)	Animal A = badger Animal B = rabbit Animal C = fox		
4 Who eats who?	**(a)**	bean plant → pigeon → cat	**(a)**	Because they make their own food
	(b)	bean plant	**(b)**	If there are not enough plants then mice will die. Then there will not be enough food for the owls which eat mice only.
	(c)	Because he eats another living thing to live		
5 How are living things adapted?	**(a)**	Mammoths had long woolly coats to keep them warm in the cold climate	**(a)**	Polar bears and arctic foxes have thick woolly coats to help keep warm/Their colours help them blend into their surroundings
	(b)	It is squirting water over its back to cool itself down	**(b)**	In a warm climate their fur would make them sweat and overheat

6 What makes you ill?	**(a)**	Linford	**(a)**	Yeast turns sugar into alcohol
	(b)	Regularly clean her teeth.	**(b)**	Heating kills the germs and stops the milk going bad
	(c)	To clean off the germs		
7 Why does food go mouldy?*	**(a)**	Germs (microbes) – accept mould	**(a)**	Spreads from germs on peoples' dirty hands or from the air.
	(b)	To protect themselves from the germs inside	**(b)**	Germs don't grow in the cold freezer because it is very cold
	(c)	Microbes		
8 What micro-organisms can you eat?	**(a)**	Yogurt, bread and blue cheese	**(a)**	It grows/eats food/makes bubbles
	(b)	To make it rise/to add bubbles to the bread	**(b)**	The dough would stop rising because the micro-organisms are killed when it is too hot

9 Can you make dirty water clean?	**(a)**	Colander and sieve are sieves Vacuum cleaner and water purifier contain filters	**(a)**	Correct order of instructions is: 1. Put the dirty water in a beaker. 2. Sieve the dirty water. 3. Put a folded filter paper in a funnel. 4. Filter the sieved water. 5. Collect the clean water in a beaker
	(b)	Colander separates vegetables from hot water in cooking Vacuum cleaner separates out the dust when cleaning. This sieve separates stones form soil in gardening Coffee filter separates out coffee grains from coffee drink		

Unit		On track: Q1		Aiming higher : Q2
10 Can you make dirty water pure?	**(a)**	Filtered pond water, lemonade and tap water are impure	**(a)**	The results match the prediction in 1(b)
	(b)	The distilled water will completely disappear. All the others will leave a deposit behind when the water evaporates.	**(b)**	Distilled water – tap water – lemonade – pond water. Order relates to the amount of solid left behind.
			(c)	Lemonade – sugar Pond water – materials from the soil Tap water- dissolved materials from reservoirs and rivers
11 How can you separate mixtures?	**(a)**	The condensed steam is clear Ink The ink will go darker blue	**(a)**	Water evaporates and steam condenses
			(b)	Salty water and tea can be separated
			(c)	I think distilled water and pure cooking oil each contain one thing because they cannot be split into different things. I think salty water contains water and salt and tea contains water and dissolved materials from the tea leaves because they can be separated.
12 What are the rules of dissolving?	**(a)**	The size of the salt crystals	**(a)**	Ignore the result and get more results to check
	(b)	Temperature or volume of water	**(b)**	Sea salt: test 2 reading of 140
			(c)	The smaller the salt crystals the faster they dissolve
13 How do we use test results?	**(a)**	Saturated solutions cannot dissolve any more solids: they are as concentrated as they can be	**(a)**	30°C – 110 g; 40°C – 120 g; 50°C – 140 g; 60°C – 160 g
			(b)	You even out the errors
	(b)	Suitable scales used on graph	**(c)**	Points drawn correctly
			(d)	130 g
14 Can changes be reversed?	**(a)**	Beaker A	**(a)**	Vinegar
	(b)	Filtering	**(b)**	Irreversible
	(c)	Sugar and water can be separated by evaporating off the water and collecting it. Sugar is left behind.	**(c)**	Gas bubbles are formed: this is a new material
15 What changes does heat cause?	**(a)**	1. Water in the saucepan heats up. 2. Water boils and turns into steam. 3. Steam mixes with the air. 4. Steam condenses on the window. It is a cold night. The window is cold helping the steam condense.	**(a)**	Cool the chocolate down
			(b)	It looks completely different/ something new has been made.
	(b)	Reversible		
16 What happens in burning?	**(a)**	The smoke is dangerous (toxic)	**(a)**	No
	(b)	The air he breathes has no oxygen and he might die	**(b)**	Water, carbon dioxide and ash
			(c)	Because new substances are formed

Unit		On track: Q1		Aiming higher : Q2
17 What is weight?	(a) (b)	Gravity The downward arrow	(a) (b) (c)	The gravity would not pull him down with as much force and so he can jump higher He would weigh less He would fall slower
18 How can you be pulled two ways?	(a) (b)	Gravity An upwards force from the seat	(a) (b) (c)	Air resistance Gravity c
19 Does weight change under water?	(a) (b)	A Newton meter Newtons	(a) (b) (c)	Upthrust 0.6 N Sink because the upthrust is less than the pull of gravity
20 What can graphs show?	(a) (b)	5 cm When a 3 N weight is put on the spring	(a) (b)	A suitable graph 10 cm
21 How do you study falling objects?	(a) (b)	Parachute D Parachute C	(a) (b)	Air resistance slows the flat piece of paper down more So they had the same weight. This makes the test fair.

Unit		On track: Q1		Aiming higher : Q2
22 How do you see things?	(a) (b)	Lamp and a TV The light goes from the TV to Linford's eyes Light goes from the lamp to the book and then to Jaden's eyes	(a) (b)	Same as drawing C The tree is not a light source in diagrams A and B the arrows should point from the light source to the tree and then to the eye in diagram D
23 What are reflections and shadows?	(a) (b)	<table><tr><td>Shadows are formed when light is blocked.</td><td>True</td></tr><tr><td>Shadows form on shiny surfaces.</td><td>False</td></tr><tr><td>Images are lifelike.</td><td>True</td></tr><tr><td>Images are formed when light is reflected.</td><td>True</td></tr><tr><td>Shadows look lifelike.</td><td>False</td></tr></table> Shadows are formed when an object blocks light. Reflections appear to be formed on shiny surfaces when light is reflected.	(a) (b)	The shadow wrongly has a lifelike face and it is a different shape to the object from which it is formed The image in the mirror is upside down rather than the right way up and it is dark rather than lifelike Correct if shadow drawn correctly, putting the above mistakes right
24 How do light beams travel?	(a) (b)	Mirror and metal spoon Polished wood or shiny plastic. Anything that is highly polished would be correct.	(a) (b) (c)	Drawing of light beam starting at the candle, zig-zagging through the periscope and hitting Asha's eyes. Arrows in the right direction. The angles are the same Mark correct if suitable diagram with arrows showing direction of the light beam.
25 How can you investigate shadows?	(a) (b)	The size of the shadow gets smaller Plot the graph with all the points marked properly and the two axes labeled correctly	(a) (b)	The bigger the distance between the light and the puppet, the smaller the shadow Mark correct if diagram showing the shadow smaller and the arrows on the light beams going in the correct direction: away from the light source

Unit		On track: Q1		Aiming higher : Q2
26 What symbols are in circuits?	**(a)** **(b)**	**a** There should be a diagonal cross in the lamp: it should not look like a plus sign **b** and **d** Neither the switch nor the connecting wires have circles on them. **c** There is a horizontal line missing in the battery between the short horizontal line and the long vertical line (e.g. see the battery symbol on page 56) Draw the symbols correctly from memory as per page 52	**(a)** **(b)**	Battery, connecting wires, buzzer, bulb The lamp lights up
27 What makes bulbs brighter?	**(a)** **(b)** **(c)**	Two cells in a battery, two bulbs and a switch. Mark correct if circuit matches those on page 58 She removed two bulbs	**(a)** **(b)** **(c)**	A cell, a switch, an electric motor and connecting wires. The second circuit is the same except she uses two cells (a battery) The motor turns Add another cell to the battery Motor
28 What makes a circuit work?	**(a)** **(b)**	The terminals of the battery are connected + – – +, and; Replacing iron wire with a piece of string Suitable circuits drawn with mistakes marked	**(a)** **(b)** **(c)** **(d)**	Switch 1 Switch 2 Switch 3 Switches 1 and 2
29 Do wires make a difference?	**(a)** **(b)**	Jaden has a prediction Linford describes what they will measure Aidan describes the factor they change Becky describes the factors they keep the same Suitable c circuit with a cell, a bulb and showing how the connecting wire can be of different lengths	**(a)** **(b)**	Suitable description explaining how the second test is fair. The thinner the wire the dimmer the bulb.

Design: Clive Sutherland

Test your knowledge

 On track

1 Asha mixed up two new substances with water.

sugar and water

sand and water

(a) In which beaker did dissolving take place?

(b) Which of these could be used to separate the sand from the water?

filtering   freezing   magnetising   melting

(c) Describe how you could reverse the mixing of sugar and water to get the sugar back.

Aiming higher

2 Next Asha added some bicarbonate of soda to a beaker of liquid. It made lots of gas bubbles. When they stopped the liquid was clear.

(a) Which liquid was Asha using?

water   oil   vinegar   wine

(b) Is the change reversible or irreversible?

(c) Which piece of evidence in the question helped you to decide on your answer to part (b)?

How well am I doing?

On track

I can describe some mixtures that can easily be separated.

Aiming higher

I can explain that changes are irreversible if a new substance is made.

15 What changes does heat cause?

- Some changes caused by heat can be reversed, and some can't.

- If a new substance is formed, the change will be hard to reverse.

Sometimes the changes caused by heating can be reversed by cooling it down, and sometimes they can't. There is no easy rule. You just need to learn a few examples of each type. A good place to start is in the kitchen – plenty of heating and cooling goes on there!

What changes due to heat can be reversed?

freezing orange juice

melting chocolate

- An orange juice lolly is just frozen orange juice. You can melt it and freeze it over and over again.

- Melted chocolate sets as it cools down. It is still chocolate.

What changes caused by heating cannot be reversed?

Cooking often changes things forever. You can't 'uncook' an egg or a cake by putting it in a fridge. Cooking doesn't just warm food up; it makes new substances that won't turn back afterwards.

Reversible

A change that can easily be undone.

Irreversible

The opposite of reversible. It can't ever be changed back.

Test your knowledge

On track

1   Some rice is boiling in water on the
    cooker. It is getting dark. Asha notices
    that there is a lot of water running down
    the inside of the cold window.

(a) Put these sentences in the right order to explain what is happening.

- Steam mixes with the air.

- Water boils and turns to steam.

- Water in the saucepan heats up.

- Steam condenses on the window.

(b) Is boiling water reversible or irreversible?

Aiming higher

2   Aidan and his mum were making some things in the kitchen. They melted some
    chocolate to pour into a mould and they boiled some eggs for their tea.

(a) Melting chocolate can be reversed quite easily. What would you have to do?

(b) What tells you that boiling an egg cannot be reversed?

How well am I doing?

On track

I can give examples of changes due to
heat that can be reversed.

Aiming higher

I can explain why changes caused by
cooking are irreversible.

16 What happens in burning?

- When materials are burnt the change cannot be reversed.
- The smoke and gases that escape are new substances.

Burning is a good example of an irreversible reaction. Once a candle burns you can never get it back again! The wax of the candle has turned into other substances such as smoke and gas, which escape into the air.

What are the dangers of burning?

You need a good supply of fresh air if you have a fire. It could use up all the oxygen you need to breathe.

Gases made by a fire are **toxic**. People caught in house fires are often poisoned by these.

What substances are formed when things burn?

When wood burns, the smoke and ash are new substances. They can't turn back to wood.

Suffocation

Dying from breathing no air with oxygen.

Toxic

Poisonous

Test your knowledge

On track

1   Bob is a fireman. You can see that he is wearing his breathing apparatus. He has a supply of air that he can use when he is near the fire.

(a) Why does he need to be protected from the smoke?

(b) What would happen if he breathed in the fumes?

Aiming higher

2   Linford's dad is burning some garden rubbish on the bonfire. His wooden wheelbarrow gets too near the flames and it gets partly burnt.

(a) The wheelbarrow was spoiled by the heat. Could it be made good again by cooling it down?

(b) What substances are formed when wood burns?

(c) Explain why the reaction cannot be reversed.

How well am I doing?

On track

I can describe some of the dangers of burning.

Aiming higher

I can explain what the production of gases tells us about burning.

17 What is weight?

- **Weight is caused by gravity pulling objects towards the centre of the Earth.**

- **Objects would have different weights on different planets.**

Imagine holding up an apple. You have to keep pushing it upwards or it will fall. The force of gravity is pulling it down. This force is also called weight. Objects weigh less on the Moon than on the Earth.

Which way does gravity pull?

Gravity is pulling the Earth and the apple towards each other.

The Earth is a ball, so 'down' is towards the middle of the Earth. Gravity pulls all objects towards the middle of the Earth.

Why do objects weigh less on the Moon?

You would get a surprise if you weighed yourself on the Moon. You would weigh much less than you do on Earth. Instead of weighing about 180 Newtons, you would only weigh about 60 Newtons. No wonder astronauts can jump so high!

The Moon is smaller than the Earth, so its pull of gravity is less.

Force

A push or a pull. Forces make things move.

Gravity

The force that pulls objects towards the centre of the Earth.

Test your knowledge

On track

1   Spot the dog jumps up to catch a stick.

(a) What force pulls Spot back to the ground?

(b) Which would be the correct arrow to add to the
     picture above to show the direction of that force?

Aiming higher

2   This astronaut is jumping on the surface of
     the Moon.

(a) How would the lower gravity change the
     height he could jump up to?

(b) What difference does the low gravity make to his weight?

(c) What would the astronaut notice about the speed he drops at?

How well am I doing?

On track

I can say what causes weight.

Aiming higher

I can describe why objects weigh less on
the Moon.

18 How can you be pulled two ways?

- Many forces can act on an object at the same time.
- The forces acting on an object can be opposite to each other.

If you push something it will move along – unless somebody else pushes it in the opposite direction! Gravity always makes something fall unless some other force is pushing it up. Why doesn't gravity make you fall down right now? Another force must be holding you up.

Why don't the clips fall?

Gravity would make the clips fall off. The magnet holds on to them with an equal force upwards.

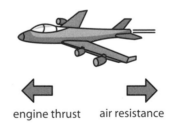

magnet pulls up

gravity pulls down

Can one force balance part of an opposite one?

The air resistance pushes against the plane as it moves through the air. The plane's shape reduces the air resistance.

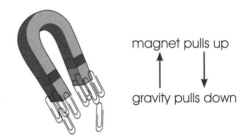

engine thrust   air resistance

Thrust

The forward force of an engine pushing a car or plane along.

Air resistance

When you run you can feel air resistance slowing you down.

Test your knowledge

On track

1   Aidan is sitting on his swing seat. He is not swinging
    – just sitting still.

(a) What is the name of the force that is pulling Aidan
     downwards?

(b) What is holding Aidan up?

Aiming higher

2   Jaden throws a paper plane
    straight ahead.

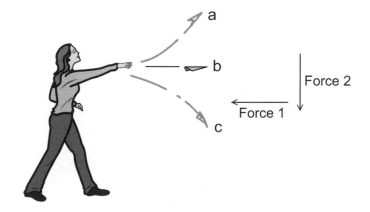

(a) What is Force 1 that is slowing
     the plane down?

(b) What is Force 2 that makes
     the plane drop?

(c) Which path will the plane
     follow: a, b or c?

How well am I doing?

On track

I can name two different forces that could
act on a moving car.

Aiming higher

I can describe how opposite forces can
balance each other.

19 Does weight change under water?

- Objects weigh less under water than they do in air.
- **If the upthrust is more than gravity, the object floats upwards.**

If you walk in a swimming pool your feet are hardly pressing on the bottom of the pool.
It seems as if you weigh almost nothing. What has happened to reduce your weight?
Gravity can still reach you in the water, so something must be holding you up.

What happens if you weigh something under water?

The reading on the
force meter shows us
that the plastic block
has a weight of 10 N.

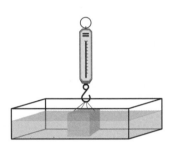

The force meter
shows us that the
metal block now has
a weight of 9 N.

Just being under water seems to make it weigh 1 N less.

The water must be pushing it upwards. That force is called **upthrust**.

Why do some objects float upwards?

These bubbles float up really fast.
The upthrust on them is much bigger
than their weight.

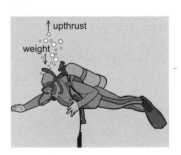

Float

Stay on the surface of a liquid
and not sink.

Upthrust

The upward force on an object
under water.

Test your knowledge

 On track

1   Linford weighs an aluminium block in air and
     in water.

(a) What is Linford using to weigh the block?

(b) What units do we use to measure weight?
     grams   newtons   centimetres   litres

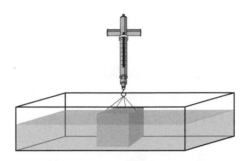

 Aiming higher

2   Here are Linford's results.
     weight of block in air   2 N
     weight of block in water   1.4 N

(a) What is the name of the upward force from the water?

(b) What is the size of the upward force?

(c) If Linford cut the string, would the block float or sink?

 How well am I doing?

On track

I can say why objects weigh less
under water.

Aiming higher

I can describe how more than one force
acts on an object at one time.

20 What can graphs show?

- You can show how an elastic band stretches with a graph.
- The graph can predict what happens if you add more weights.

You know that a spring or an elastic band will stretch if you pull them. The harder you pull, the more they stretch. We can measure that scientifically and show our results on a graph. You can do it yourself with some simple equipment.

How does an elastic band stretch as you add weights to it?

Method

- Jaden measured the length of the band without any weights on it. She added a 1 N weight and measured it again.
- She added more weights and measured the length of the band each time.

Results

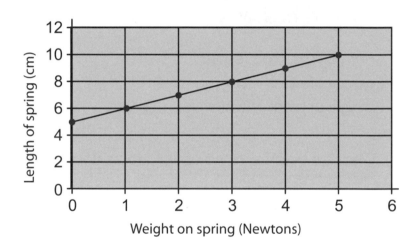

What can a graph show?

Jaden's graph shows a **pattern**. She says,

'The more weights you add the longer the band becomes.'

She adds, 'It lets you predict readings. You can see that a weight of 3.5 N would stretch the band to 8.25 cm.'

Line graph

A graph where the points are joined up by a line.

Newton or N

The scientific unit used to measure weight.

Test your knowledge

On track

1   Jaden studied how much
    a spring stretches when she
    hung weights on it.
    This graph shows her results.

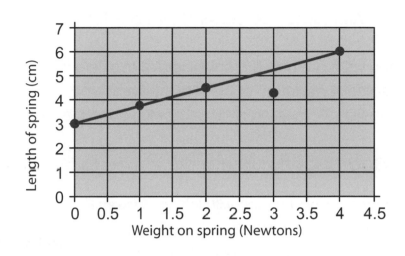

(a) What is the length of the
    spring without any weight
    on it?

(b) Which of Jaden's readings
    looks odd and is probably
    wrong?

Aiming higher

2   Here is another set of results for a different spring.

Weight on spring (N)	Length of spring (cm)
0	5
10	7
20	9
30	11
40	13
50	15

(a) Make a graph of these results on a separate piece of graph paper. Plot the weight
    results on the horizontal (x) axis.

(b) What length would the spring be if a weight of 25 N was put on it?

How well am I doing?

On track

I can read a graph showing a
spring stretching.

Aiming higher

I can use a graph to make predictions.

21 How do you study falling objects?

- The shape of a piece of paper affects how fast it falls.
- Air resistance slows down a falling piece of paper.

You will know that different things fall at different speeds. A brick lands much sooner than a feather if you let go of them at the same time. The force of gravity should make them fall together. Something must be slowing down the feather.

Does shape make a difference to how fast things fall?

Tiger class had a race with letting different shapes of paper fall. They started off with a lot of pieces of A4 paper. They all had to be the same size so the test was fair. They made them into different shapes and dropped them all from the same height.

Drop all the pieces of paper all at the same time. See which one hits the ground first.

flat paper	slowest
paper folded in half	second slowest
screwed-up paper	second fastest
paper carefully folded to be small	fastest

Here are the class results.

What is the best explanation?

There are lots of things to think about.
- Do the pieces of paper weigh the same?
- Does gravity pull each piece equally?
- Does air have much upthrust on paper?
- What could be slowing the paper down?

The only really important thing is air resistance. A larger piece of paper has more air resistance, rather like a parachute. The tightly-folded paper is able to move more quickly through the air because it small.

The pieces of paper were the same size and weight to start with, to make the test fair.

Explanation
The scientific reason that something has happened.

Fair test
Only testing one idea or factor at a time.

Test your knowledge

On track

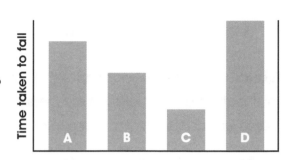

1 Paul timed how long it took for different parachutes to fall.

(a) Which parachute took the longest time to fall?

(b) Which was the smallest parachute?

Aiming higher

2 Tiger class are discussing why a flat piece of paper fell much more slowly than a screwed-up piece.

(a) Write down the explanation which you think is true.

Gravity pulls the fast pieces down more strongly.

Paper folded up small has less upthrust.

The flat piece fell slowly because it weighed less.

Air resistance slows the flat piece of paper down more.

(b) Why was it important for both pieces of paper to be the same size before one was screwed up?

How well am I doing?

On track

I can find out what shapes of paper fall fastest.

Aiming higher

I can give a reason why different pieces of paper fall at different speeds.

22 How do you see things?

- You see something when light from it enters your eyes.
- Drawings of light beams help to explain how you see things.

Candle flames, light bulbs and the Sun are all light sources. Light beams travel from them in straight lines. Sometimes the beams go straight into your eyes. At other times they hit an object, bounce off, and then enter your eyes.

Why do we see light sources?

Linford remembered that light sources, such as a candle flame, give off light.

He knew that he would see this candle flame when light from it entered his eyes.

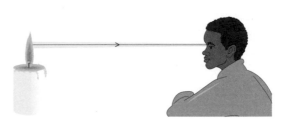

How do light beams help you explain how you see things?

Miss Harper asked Aidan how he could see an object which didn't give off light. He drew a diagram to illustrate his explanation and said: 'You would only see this object if there was a light source as well. Light from the source would bounce off the object and then enter your eyes. The arrow in the centre of the light beam shows the direction it travels. We always draw it at the centre - this is the rule.'

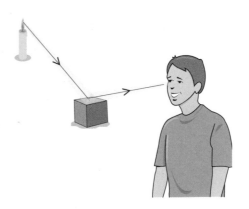

Light source

An object that gives off light.

Light beam

A ray of light travelling in a straight line.

Test your knowledge

On track

1   There is one big mistake in each of
    these diagrams.

(a) Name the sources of light in each of
    these diagrams.

(b) Explain what is wrong in each picture.

Aiming higher

2   Four children think they know how Jaden sees a tree.

      A   **B**   **C**   **D**

(a) Draw the diagram of the light beam which shows how she sees the tree.

(b) Explain why the other diagrams are wrong.

How well am I doing?

On track

I can describe how light lets us see things.

Aiming higher

I can use drawings of light beams to
explain how we see things.

23 What are reflections and shadows?

- Reflections (images) and shadows are formed in different ways.
- **Reflections and shadows look completely different.**

Shadows and reflections are different. Shadows are made when an object blocks the light. Reflections are formed when light bounces off a shiny surface.

How are reflections and shadows formed?

Jaden looks at her image in the mirror. Light beams hit her face, travel to the mirror and are reflected back into her eyes. She can see every detail of her face in the image in the mirror.

Jaden's shadow is formed when her body blocks the light from the torch. No light travels back from the shadow so it looks dark.

How do reflections and shadows differ?

- Reflections in a mirror look lifelike. You can see every detail (even the colours).
- Shadows are dark places. They just have the shape of their object.

Image
A lifelike likeness of an object produced by a shiny surface.

Shadow
A dark outline of an object formed when light is blocked.

Test your knowledge

On track

1   Here are some statements about shadows and images.

(a) Decide if each statement is true or false. Copy the table and complete it.

Statement	True or False
Shadows are formed when light is blocked.	
Shadows form on shiny surfaces.	
Images are lifelike.	
Images are formed when light is reflected.	
Shadows look lifelike.	

(b) Explain in your own words how a shadow and reflection are formed.

Aiming higher

2   Look at these two drawings. Spot what is wrong!

(a) Name two things which are wrong in each drawing.

(b) Draw the shadow in (a) correctly.

How well am I doing?

On track

I can say how reflections and shadows are formed.

Aiming higher

I can describe the differences between shadows and reflections.

24 How do light beams travel?

- When light hits a shiny surface it is **reflected**.

- **Beams of light change direction when they are reflected.**

When a beam of light from an object hits a mirror it bounces off. The light has been reflected. You will see the object if the beam enters your eye. The angle at which a beam hits a mirror is the same as the one that bounces off.

What happens when light hits a shiny surface?

Asha can see an image of the candle in the mirror. This is because light from the candle hits the mirror, is reflected and enters her eye.

Beams of light come from different parts of the candle. When they enter her eye they make a lifelike image.

How does the light beam travel?

Asha explains.

'The beam travels from the light source to the mirror in a straight line and hits it at an angle. It is reflected (bounced off) at the same angle.'

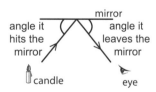

Image

A lifelike representation of a person, animal or thing.

Periscope

An optical instrument for seeing things that are higher up or obstructed.

Test your knowledge

On track

1   Look at these four different objects.

mirror   plastic spoon   metal spoon   paper

(a) Which two objects in this list would reflect light well?

(b) Name two other materials that would reflect light well.

Aiming higher

Asha can see the lamp by looking through her periscope. It has two mirrors inside. One at the top and one at the bottom.

(a) Draw the light beam that goes from the candle to Asha's eye.

(b) What can you say about the two angles formed when the beam hits each mirror?

(c) Draw a diagram showing how a mirror could be used to see around corners.

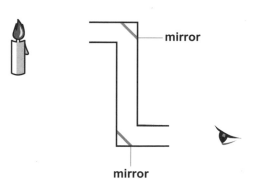

How well am I doing?

On track

I can use light beams to explain how images are formed.

Aiming higher

I can predict the angle at which a light beam will bounce.

25 How can you investigate shadows?

- Fair tests help you investigate how shadows change.
- You can make sense of these tests using beams of light.

Shadows can change in size. Moving a light source nearer to an object makes the shadow bigger. Moving the light source further away makes the shadow smaller. You can find out how this works by doing a fair test, plotting graphs and drawing some ray diagrams.

How did Linford investigate the size of shadows?

Linford made shadows of his puppet on the screen. He noticed that the shadow changed size if he moved the light. He decided to investigate this properly with a fair test.

I changed how near the light was to the puppet and measured the height of the shadow.

To make my test fair I kept the distance between the puppet and the screen the same all the time.

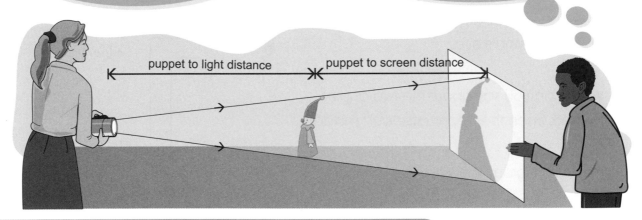

puppet to light distance   puppet to screen distance

How can he make sense of his investigation?

Now he can do two things. He can:

- look at his results carefully to see if he can find a rule;
- try to explain this using beams of light like those in the drawing.

Convention

An agreed way of doing something.

Rule

A sentence which sums up a pattern.

Test your knowledge

On track

1 What happens to the size of the shadow if he keeps the puppet and the screen the same and moves the torch further away?.

Distance between the torch and the puppet (cm)	20	40	60	80	100
Height of the shadow (cm)	95	50	31	24	20

(a) What happens to the size of the shadow if he keeps the shadow the same and moves the torch further away?

(b) Plot the points then draw a line graph of his results, putting the distance from the light to puppet on the *x* axis (along the bottom).

Aiming higher

2 Look at the pattern in your graph.

(a) Pick the right rule from this list.

- The bigger the distance between the light and the puppet, the bigger the shadow.
- Moving the light makes no difference to the size of the shadow.
- The bigger the distance between the light and the puppet, the smaller the shadow.

(b) To show that you understand the rule, draw one ray diagram like the one on page 54 but with the light further away from the puppet.

How well am I doing?

On track

I can describe how to test to see how shadows change.

Aiming higher

I can use light beams to show how the size of shadows change.

26 What symbols are in circuits?

- Each electrical component has a special symbol.
- You can draw electrical circuits using these special symbols.

Cells, bulbs and wires each have their own special symbol. You can use them to draw diagrams of circuits in a very clear way. This helps you understand them and to build your own.

What are the correct symbols for some common components?

These symbols have to be drawn exactly the same every time you use them.

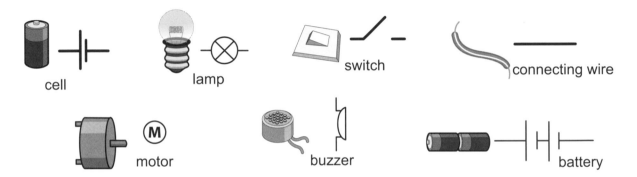

cell   lamp   switch   connecting wire

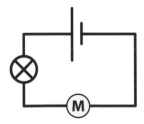

motor   buzzer   battery

How can the symbols be used to draw simple circuits?

Here are two examples. Both of them have been drawn using the correct symbols.

This circuit has one cell, one bulb and a motor. The circuit is complete and both the motor and bulb are working.

This circuit has one cell, one bulb and a switch. When the switch is closed, the circuit is complete and the bulb lights up.

Circuit diagram

A drawing which shows you how a circuit is connected.

Symbol

A simple diagram which represents part of a circuit.

Test your knowledge

On track

1   These symbols have all been
    drawn in the wrong way.

(a) Explain what is wrong with
    each symbol.

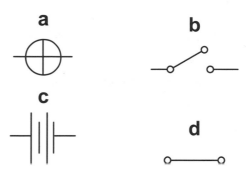

(b) Draw and label each one correctly.

Aiming higher

2   Look at this drawing of a more
    complicated circuit.

(a) Name the components in this circuit.

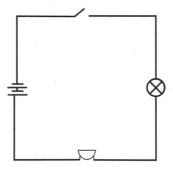

(b) When the switch is closed, the buzzer
    sounds. What else happens?

How well am I doing?

On track

I can draw a circuit using the
correct symbols.

Aiming higher

I can recognise the components in an
unfamiliar circuit.

27 What makes bulbs brighter?

- Circuits work best when each component has enough power to work.
- **The brightness of bulbs or speed of motors can be changed.**

You can get switches that make lights brigher or dimmer. In the circuits you use, bulbs will glow brighter in a circuit if you use more cells on fewer bulbs. The same idea works with motors or buzzers.

Why were the lights in Jaden's lighthouse at normal brightness?

Jaden's lighthouse has a battery of two cells and two bulbs. The lights go on and off when you open and close the switch.

The two cells give the two bulbs just the right amount of electricity.

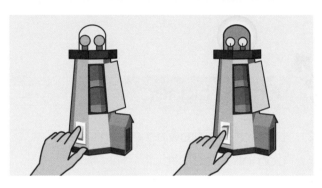

How can we make bulbs brighter or dimmer?

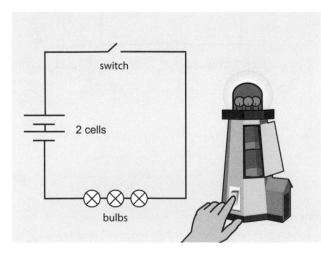

The extra bulb makes them all dimmer.

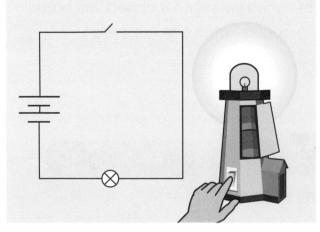

With one bulb removed, the other one is much brigher.

Component	Cell
The parts of an electrical circuit (wires, bulbs and lamp, etc.).	A component used in a circuit which supplies electricity.

Test your knowledge

On track

1   Jaden could choose from these
    compounds to build her lighthouses.
    She did not need them all.

(a) Which components did she actually
    use in her circuit?

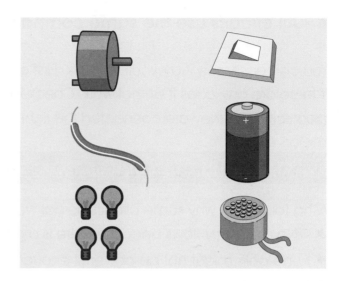

(b) Draw her lighthouse circuit using the
    correct symbols.

Look at Jaden's circuits on the previous page.

(c) What did she do to change the brightness of the bulb?

Aiming higher

2   Jaden built these two circuits to make
    a merry-go-round.

(a) Name the components used to make
    each circuit.

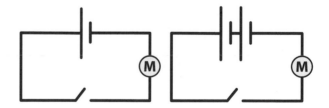

(b) What will happen in each circuit when
    the switch is closed?

(c) What would you do to make the merry-
    go-round go really fast?

(d) What part of the circuit is connected to
    the merry-go-round to make it move?

How well am I doing?

On track

I can describe how to make a bulb light to
normal brightness.

Aiming higher

I can explain how to change the brightness
of bulbs or speed of motors.

28 What makes a circuit work?

- Circuits might not work for a variety of reasons.
- All circuits use the same components as the ones you know.

You can easily see if a circuit will work. First check to see if there is a complete circuit. If there are any gaps it will not work. Check to see that all the components conduct electricity and they are connected the right way round.

What might stop a circuit from working?

Asha found out why some circuits do not work.

- No electricity flows because there is a gap in the circuit or a component is broken.
- The cells might not be powerful enough to make the circuit work.
- The cells might be too powerful, burning out some of the components.
- The battery won't work because the +ve or –ve terminals of each cell touch each other.

Does this unfamiliar circuit work?

Asha builds a 'steady hand' game.

The idea is to move the ring along the curly wire from one end to the other without making the buzzer and light come on.

There is nothing in this circuit to stop it working. It is complete, the cells in the battery are connected correctly, there is enough power and all the components work.

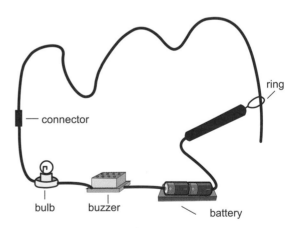

You can draw this circuit using the normal symbols for electrical components.

Circuit

A path for electricity to flow.

Terminal

The positive (+) or negative (–) ends of a cell.

Test your knowledge

On track

1   Asha has made a number of circuits, some worked and some did not.

(a) Which of these would stop a circuit working?

    (i)   The terminals of the battery are connected +−+−.

    (ii)   The terminals of the battery are connected +− −+.

    (iii) Replacing the iron wire with a piece of string.

    (iv) Replacing the iron wire with gold wire.

(b) Draw two circuits of your own that do not work. Label them to show why they do not work.

Aiming higher

2   Asha builds a circuit to work just like traffic lights do.

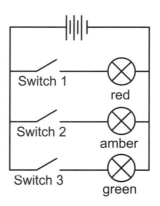

(a) What switch(es) should she press down to make just the red light come on?

(b) What switch(es) should she press down to make just the amber light come on?

(c) What switch(es) should she press down to make just the green light come on?

(d) What switch(es) should she press down to make the red and amber lights come on?

How well am I doing?

On track

I can say what is needed to make a circuit work.

Aiming higher

I can understand an unfamiliar circuit.

29 Do wires make a difference?

- Circuits can show how different wires change a bulb's brightness.

- **Comparisons of a bulb's brightness help to produce a rule.**

Circuit wires come in different thicknesses and lengths. The brightness of bulbs can be altered by changing wires in a circuit. You can try fair tests with different wires. Your results will help you come up with a rule.

What did Tiger class investigate?

Miss Harper asked the class a question: 'Does the length of a wire in a circuit alter the brightness of a bulb?'

She asked the pupils to think how they might test this. Before they started they had a discussion about their plan and what they might do.

They could use these components.

What results did they get?

Asha says, 'We can make our test fair if we compare the brightness of the same bulb in a circuit which has different lengths of the same wire.'

This is what they found out. The results show a pattern.

Length of wire (m)	2	10	20	30
Brightness of the bulb	very bright	bright	dimmer than normal	very dim
What was the pattern?				

Linford came up with a rule: 'The longer the wire the dimmer the bulb is.'

Rule	Wire
A statement which sums up a pattern.	A thin length of metal which conducts electricity.

Test your knowledge

 **On track**

1   Here are some ideas that Tiger class came up when thinking about their fair test.

> I think the longer wire will make the bulb dimmer.

Jaden says

> Let's record the brightness of the bulbs in the different circuits.

Linford says

> Use different lengths of the same wire.

Aidan says

> Always use the same cell, bulb and switch in each circuit.

Asha says

(a) What is each pupil describing?

The factor they keep the same   What they will measure

A prediction   The factor they change

(b) Draw the circuit, using the correct symbols, that they use.

 Aiming higher

2   Tiger class then tested wires of different thickness in the same circuit. Here are their results.

Thickness of wire (mm)	5	4	3	2	1
Brightness of bulb	very bright	bright	normal brightness	dimmer than normal	very dim

(a) Describe how you would do this fair test.

(b) What rule does the results show?

 How well am I doing?

On track   **Aiming higher**

I can set up a circuit to investigate an idea.   I can use results to come up with a rule.

Index